I0424112

Learn How To Sexting

Learn How To Sexting
Texting guide for women dating men

THOMAS VUM

Contents

Introduction

To sext is to meet your partner in a portable private classroom — a place where you communicate your needs and desires — so by the time you're in bed together, you know each others' deepest fantasies without having to say a word. Our smart phones give us permission to dream big and dare to dream with another person.

Of course, trust is essential. You probably don't want to engage in an intimate and explicit conversation with a guy who shortly after exchanging numbers requests a picture of your private parts or any idiot who sends you a Snapchat of his private part after only a few brief exchanges. Bad sexters are like bad lovers — a huge disappointment. But they shouldn't turn you off to the act entirely.

Good sexters know that the advantage to putting our thoughts into words is that we can stop, think, edit, or erase entirely. We have time. And it's often time that is the biggest turn-on. While de we used to be very patient for emails replies, now our anticipation peaks within a few minutes.

How arousing it is to watch that gray bubble, its row of three periods pulsing, telling you that your guy has re-thought his text, erased it, is perhaps biting his lip, designing the perfect phrase, or filtering the hottest picture before he finally hits Send.

This book contains proven steps and strategies on how to sext for women. Give these tips a good try and enjoy the ride along the way.

Chapter 1

Be aware

Before you embark on sexting, you need to take serious precautions. In 2014, hundreds of thousands of Snapchat photos were leaked online in a leak dubbed the 'Snappening'. In the same year, hundreds of celebrity photos were also leaked. This underlines the importance of taking precautions before sending any nude, or semi nude photos online.

These precautions cannot guarantee that your images will never be leaked. However, you are more secure than not taking precautions at all. In fact, if you follow these precautions, then you don't need to worry about anything at all.

1. **Use Anti-Theft App On Your Phone**

   If you are actively sexting, this needs to go beyond your usual screen lock. Your phone can be stolen and you will need to ensure that strangers don't get hold of the phone and begin sending your photos to random people online. This can come back to hurt you as people tend to widely share a lot of embarrassing photos for their own amusement.

There are ways you can prevent this. If you are using an android phone, an android device manager can be set up in such a way that you can erase or lock the phone remotely. You can also change the password remotely.

There are also similar apps on an IOS device. All you have to do is to find suitable software that allows you to change password, or erase the photos remotely.

2. Use Sobriety Apps

Most women will likely send nudes and texts they otherwise wouldn't have sent, if they've hadn't too much to drink. It is always advisable not to call, text and most importantly, sext, when you're tipsy or drunk. There is a very good chance that it will be too embarrassing to share when you're finally sober.

There are also apps that you can download, if you feel you don't have the discipline to control yourself. These apps are sobriety apps that check on how sober you are before they allow you to text.

Webroot is a popular sobriety test app that can be downloaded from both the IOS and Android store. You may activate the app before you go on a night out, just to make sure you'll not be sending text to an ex, or the guy you recently met.

Additionally, there are apps that have features that make them ideal for sexting. There are Apps that will self destruct after a set period of time. There are also apps that have features that only allow messaging between couples. Screenshot protection is another important feature that prevents the other party from taking screen shots and sharing them online.

To get a list of apps with these features you may do a simple Google search for "sexting apps". There is a wide range of apps you could choose for more secure sexting.

3. Text Instead

The other precaution you can take is to text, instead of sending images. Photos can leave a more embarrassing image of you floating online. They are also considered to be more authentic, since it is easier to create a fake text screenshot than to do sophisticated image manipulations on someone's photos.

Relationship experts also advice against sending nudes at the early stages of your relationship. Unless you're in a serious relationship, it is advisable to wait until much later, when you're both comfortable with each other.

4. Don't Save

You can make it a rule between you and your partner not to save any steamy texts or photos. Most people sext as a prelude to an actual sexual encounter. So you may text him just before you meet him later on that night.

After the whole encounter is over, you need to delete the messages. Sometimes these messages are never uploaded online by any of the spouses. Snooping friends have been known to upload them. So no matter how much you trust each other, you need to delete the images as soon as you can.

5. Avoid Sexting on Your Work phone

Sexting on your work phone, needless to say, is a very bad idea. There are many things that can go wrong, if you chose to use your work phone. You can accidentally send the messages to your boss.

It is also possible that other people in your social circle, particularly colleagues at work, may feel less reserved in going through your phone, if they realize it is your work phone. Whether you believe it is okay for them to do that or not, make sure you use your own private phone. This must be a phone you do not share with anyone else.

6. Do Not Disclose Details

Another very important precaution you must take is to avoid giving out details. This includes names, addresses, locations and anything that may disclose the identity of the person sending the message, or the one receiving it.

You should also sit down with your partner and agree not to share any private information on the platform you are using. Using applications can give higher levels of privacy than normal GSM text messaging. You can always use applications that hide your ID, so that it is impossible to trace the message back to you.

Chapter 2

Let's get started

Once you've taken the necessary precautions, it is time to get your hands dirty. But you need to know that there is always the right way and the right time to do it. Here are tips you can make use of to ensure that you make the most of the moment.

1. **Xrated Can Be A Turn Off**

   It is assumed that men like no-holds-barred sex. It is a common belief that men like to talk dirty and therefore wouldn't mind X-rated images and texts. However, there are things that you'll need to consider, before you begin sending x-rated sexts.

   According to some studies over 30% of men don't like x-rated images. They prefer more subtle images of sex and other means of sexual expression. You need to know your man before you can send hardcore messages. Be on the safe side and send messages that are more subtle and direct.

2. Meet First – Best When You Know Someone Well Enough

It may seem obvious to state that you should never sext to someone you just met. Apparently, there are people who have done this a number of times: most of the time the results are not what they expected.

It is best to take time to know the person you want to sext to. It can be awkward to do it with someone you just met. It may probably be more awkward for him than it is for you, and you may only realize this when it's too late.

3. Wait Till You've Done 'It'

Relationship expert also advise couples to wait till they've had some sexual encounter with their partners. Before that, one or probably both of you may feel uneasy. The truth is no one wants to feel pushed into something they are not prepared to do.

If you've not had sex or any form of sexual encounter, it is best to only send innocent flirtatious texts if anything: don't engage in any form of sexting or send nude or seminude images beforehand.

4. Not At Work

You need to ensure the mood is right before you can send any text to your partner. You must therefore ensure that you do it at the right time in the right place. If he is at work that may not be an ideal time to begin initiating a sexting session.

Alternatively, you can send softer more mysterious messages, to indicate that you're in the mood for some action later on in the night. This type of message shouldn't be too straight forward. It could be something like *"Hoping to see you later, I have a little surprise for you."*

5. Find Out The Best Time To Do It

You need to find out if that is the best time to engage in some steamy sexting. You shouldn't just start sending messages from the blue. Send an initial message first that will help you figure out what that person is up to.

Don't send a message without warning, particularly if you're not sure whether he is still at work or not. You can send a sexy message like *"Are you alone tonight? Want to play a game"*. This gives the cue about what you're intentions are and serves as a warning in case your partner is in the middle of work.

6. Don't Be Overeager

After sending an initial message, you may be very eager to send some more messages, even before you get a response. Sending multiple messages to your partner without any response can seem desperate. It is easy to turn of your partner if he feels you're being desperate, especially when he is not in the mood.

Therefore this can be a very big mistake. The advisable thing to do is to avoid sending a string of messages, until you get a positive response.

It is also important to emphasize being yourself. Even though you can use examples you find online, don't try to act like someone else, unless it is a role play session you're having with your partner.

One way you can tell if you're not being yourself is if you feel awkward. Avoid anything that makes you feel uneasy. This is a simple rule that should be observed for any kind of romantic or sexual encounter.

7. Foreplay

One way you can make the experience more intense for both of you is to think of sexting as foreplay. Think of it as part of the main thing: when both of you are lustful, sexting can be quite intense and pleasurable. The key is to sustain the intensity of the moment 'till both of you meet later in the night.

If done right, it may prove to be worth it once both of you meet later in the night. Because it is part of foreplay, you can take advantage of that and use it to communicate what you want. Make suggestions and be flirtatious. Use your imagination and make the most of it.

8. Build Up Sexual Chemistry

Instead of rushing into it, let the whole thing build up spontaneously. You need to mirror the direction your partner is heading. Sometimes, he may choose to be more intense. Raise the sexual intensity of your text, but make sure you don't go overboard.

Taking time to intuitively find out the other person's intensions can help to not only build up sexual tension, but learn your partner better. This is definitely an advantage for both of your sex lives.

9. Get Dirty

Even though relationship experts say it is advisable to avoid the X-rated stuff, there comes a time when it may be okay to start pushing the boundaries.

According to relationship experts, couples who talk dirty tend to be more open with each other. According to these experts, communication between couples that engage in dirty sex talk is often open. Perhaps this is a result of shedding inhibitions. Couples feel free to talk to each other about their feelings.

The rule is to keep avoid sending lots of steamy message without warning. Send the first message and structure it such that it serves as a warning for the messages to come later.

10. Do It Sparingly

Talking dirty can make the sexting session between the two of you very intense. It can serve as a build up for a hot romantic encounter later on. But you have to do it right.

The rule is to do it more spontaneously and sparingly. Avoid sending messages immediately. Sending dirty sex messages all the time will soon become boring and predictable. Be a little more mysterious and intuitive. Take time to learn of your partner's feelings and what he wants.

11. Keep It Classy

Another thing you must do is to keep it classy. Be mysterious and don't simply state your desires directly. If you're with a new partner, try to be poetic and a little sentimental. This gives you time to gauge the kind of messages that would turn him on, or put him off.

This also involves taking time to try and understand if your partner will appreciate steamy text messages. Avoid getting too dirty, especially with a new partner.

12. Role Play

Since sexting is often a prelude for a sexual encounter. You can always incorporate other things that you like to do or to be done to you in the bedroom. One of the things that you can incorporate is role play. If you and your partner enjoy role playing sex games, then there is no reason why you can't incorporate into sexting.

Role play opens up sexting to more ideas. It is one of the best forms of sexting for people who are a little shy with being direct with what they want to sext. There are lots of ideas you can get by making a simple search online.

13. Communicate Your Desires

It is easy to focus on pleasing your partner. However, you should remember that you are part of the relationship and your desires also count.

In fact, this is one of the best ways you can communicate your desires without being straight forward. You can use the opportunity to indicate your preferred sex position. You can also use it to emphasize that you need him to focus on oral sex. Whatever it is you want this is one of the best ways to communicate that desire.

14. Images

You can always send images of you in your nude and semi nude state. However, as we discussed earlier, this can be risky. Many jilted boyfriends and girlfriends have leaked these images online.

There are many sexy images available online that you can send to spice you text messages. There is no rule that says the messages must be yours. There are sex position stock photos as, well as celebrity sex scenes from R and X rated movies. All these images are free to use and are risk free. You can find whatever you want; it all depends on your imagination.

15. Read A Lot

If you do not have a clear idea of the kind of messages you can send, all you need to do is to look at sexting messages shared online.

These are suggestions from relationship experts and people who have a lot of experience sending these messages.

These messages can help you the tone intensity and structure of the sexts that you send. There are those that are very subtle, while others are more direct and dirty. All you have to do is to enter the phrase *"Sexting examples."*

Chapter 3

The Don'ts

You have set up everything and you are now engaging in a lustful sexting session with your partner. You need to watch out for those things that can ruin the moment and leave you feeling awkward or guilty. Taking a few precautions can help you to avoid some of these awkward situations.

1. **Don't Be Sloppy**

   You shouldn't take sexting too seriously. However, this does not mean that you get sloppy with the kind of messages you send. Always make a point of ensuring that the message is comprehensible.

   Using short codes or words that the other person does not understand can ruin an otherwise intense sexting session. Make a point of learning whether your partner understands you. Also avoid the shortened words, unless they are words you use often.

Check for spelling, even if you have to use a spell checker.

2. Don't Give Too Much Away

You shouldn't give too much away in your messages. You should communicate your intentions, but not in a way that is too direct. Like we have mentioned in the tips above, this is important for new couples.

Couples that have been together for long, or are married, can break most of the rules here. However, younger couples need to be more cautious before making any bold moves.

3. Don't Sext If You Haven't Done The Thing

Another important rule for young couples to follow is never to sext before sexual encounter happens. Even when it does, it is still important for the couples to be more subtle, when sending the messages. The two can always explore further, once they get to know each other's sexual preferences better.

4. Don't Sext What You Wouldn't Say In Real Life

This is an important rule for those who do not know what to text. As mentioned in the previous tip, it is important to wait until you're comfortable with your partner, before you can send any bold X rated messages.

One way to find out if the messages you're sending are appropriate is by following this rule. Think if you would say out loud to your partner what you're about to text. If you can't, then you probably shouldn't send the message to him.

5. Don't Be Discouraged By Discomfort

It is going to be uncomfortable for the first few times. For many people, this discomfort wears off after sometime. For others, it may take longer before they can overcome the anxiety or discomfort. However, it always gets better with time.

You shouldn't let the discomfort take over you and prevent you from having this thrilling encounter with your partner.

Some women may feel that talking dirty and submission contradicts feminism. However, this is definitely not the case. Dirty talk and submission in the bedroom are similar to role play. It is simply involves playing out roles that you otherwise wouldn't outside of the bedroom.

6. Don't Expect To Get It Right The First Time

You shouldn't expect to get sexting right the first dozen times you try it. In fact, probably no one ever gets it right all the time. Even those who have been doing it for years do get anxious and will feel a little strange every time they do it with new partners.

The rule is to always start with more subtle and understated messages. You can always progress to more hardcore messages later. Avoid sending images, unless you know your partner well enough.

7. Don't Feel Guilty

If you feel guilty or awkward after sending the sext messages, you need to remind yourself that there is nothing wrong with what you're doing. There is no moral or ethical reason that should justify any ounce of guilt you allow in your being simply for texting.

Guilt can ruin sexual interaction developing between you and your boyfriend. This breeds inhibitions and reluctance on the part of the person who feels guilty. Feeling awkward can make it harder for you to communicate what you're feeling to your partner.

8. Don't Overlook Precautions

It is always wise to follow the precautions that have been listed in other sections of this book. In fact, you should make it a rule to follow these precautions before you do any serious texting.

Later on in the relationship, when both of you have more intense sexting sessions, you should also make sure that your partner is also paying attention to these precautions. Make a point of having both of your phones installed with the anti-theft application.

9. Don't Do It For any Other Reason

You should not sext for any other reason but for fun and for the thrill of it. It is still possible, even as an adult, to feel pressured to try out sexting because your friends are doing it, or your partner insists on it.

Never succumb to any form of pressure. Sexting under any form of psychological pressure can affect your sex life. You may start to feel uneasy about having any form of sexual contact with your partner, as a result of feeling cheated.

Always communicate your feelings. Make a point of turning down any form of suggestion that makes you feel uncomfortable. Most importantly you need to rethink your relationship with anyone who may try to pressure you to send sext messages.

Chapter 4

Further more

Several leaked messages and images of high profile politicians have made sexting more popular in recent times. This is not the first time that people are sending their partners these messages. Even with the advent of the mobile phones and internet, there were quite a number of steamy messages that were being shared on different platforms back at the time. These messages were never taken seriously, until messages started getting leaked online.

In 2014, hackers announced that they had released naked photos of celebrities online. This was later followed by what was referred to as the "snappening". Thousands of snapchat photos were leaked online. Since snap chat is one of the popular sexting app, these photos were sext messages from ordinary people.

It is these events that have led to a lot of shame and stigma to be associated with sexting. Studies have shown that more people have continued to associate sexting with shame and embarrassment. A lot of people will feel embarrassed, if their photos are leaked online.

However, there are other interesting facts that indicate that many people have engaged in some form of sexting at one point in their lives. This is particularly true for those in their 30s and 40s, who are still very tech savvy.

According to this study 67% of undergraduates had engaged in some form of sexting. Sometimes women sent these messages more than men. Men who received more messages than they sent often had more than one sexual partner.

More importantly, the studies showed how these 'leaks' tend to shape what we consider appropriate. As more and more photos and messages were leaked online, more people began to view sexting as a negative thing; something that is likely to bring shame and embarrassment to those who engaged in it.

The question then is whether you should engage in sexting. This question has many answers depending on the person who is asking it. Some people have a very high threshold for anything that may be considered awkward. It is important to reflect on your personality before you can begin sexting.

If you're shy, it is easy for you to feel awkward. Sometimes this can ruin a good sexting session between you and your partner. People with this type of personality need to take time before they can jump into the deep end of sexting. Short suggestive messages should be enough for those who are trying out sexting. Later on you can try out something more explicit and sexual.

How well do you know your partner? This is an important question to reflect on because it has many implications. Getting to know your partner can help you determine, if the messages you are sending are appropriate. If you don't know your partner well enough, then play it safe and avoid messages that may seem over the top.

It is also important to know your partner because this can help you to gauge how suitable they are for sexting. If you feel pressured to sext, then avoid doing it altogether. A partner who pushes you to send some of these messages is probably not even a good match for you.

This is one reason why it is important to take time before you begin sending a string of messages to someone who you just met recently. Taking time lets you gauge whether they are trustworthy. If you ever feel uncomfortable avoid doing it altogether.

Last but not least, ensure that you take all the necessary precautions. Most of the precautions are just simple steps like installing the right apps and this will only take a few minutes. Once you take all the advice here, there is no reason why you won't be safe. You can now do it without worry. Make the most of it and enjoy.